Hey Babysitter, Let's Play!

A Guide to
Fun and Games
for Babysitters

™Ⓡ

By Gwen Bockman and Jana Fitting

Hey Babysitter, Let's Play!

A Guide to Fun and Games for Babysitters

InQuisitors (InQ) Publishing Co.
P.O. Box 10
North Aurora, Illinois 60542-0010

Copyright© 1990 by Jana Sue Fitting and Gwen Bockman
First Printing 1990
Second Printing 1991
Printed in the United States of America

Library of Congress Card Number: 89-84492

ISBN 0-923889-57-4 (paperback)
ISBN 0-923889-64-7 (spiral)

DEDICATION

To our husbands and children we give special thanks for your support, thoughts and participation in helping to create this book of fun!

———————————————

This is our gift of fun to children everywhere!

ACKNOWLEDGEMENT

Many friends, family members and specialists have given us advice, help and support in this project. We thank you all!

Special contributions:

      Bobette Wolf, Wolf Design
      Jere Nelson, inside illustrations
      Rebecca Ryan, cover characters

ABOUT THE AUTHORS

Gwen Bockman is the mother of two children and an experienced teacher of preschool and elementary students. She has been involved in developing educational programs throughout her career. She has been recognized as a "Top Teacher" by her former students and their parents.

Jana Fitting is the author of **A Magical Piece of Sand**, a young children's book that features "visually active typography". She is active in organizing and working with children through school, church and community groups, and is the mother of three sons.

NOTICE

The games, activities and information included in this book are accurate and complete to the best of our knowledge. Much effort has been taken to insure that these games and activities can be successfully used in the safest manner by babysitters with varying amounts of experience. However no guarantee is made on the part of the authors or InQuisitors Publishing Co. The authors and publisher disclaim all liability incurred in connection with the use of the information in this book.

Dear Parents!

We hope you enjoy using *HEY BABYSITTER, LET'S PLAY!* It is as much for you as for the babysitter. Set this book out for the babysitter to select activities while you are away. You may prefer to choose the activities and provide the necessary materials for your babysitter. You may even enjoy playing these activities with your child.

However you choose to use it, this is meant to be the starting place for FUN!

Read — use — and enjoy!

TABLE OF CONTENTS

HEY BABYSITTER,

This is a guide to fun and games written especially for you. In this book you will find games and activities for you to do with infants through young school-age children. Taking *HEY BABYSITTER, LET'S PLAY!* along with you on each job can help create lots of fun for you and the child.

To help you decide which activities each child will enjoy most, a picture code representing the child's skill level is included. For those interested in educational play, key values (denoted as E.V. for educational value) are also listed and defined in the glossary. Both are listed with each activity.

As a good babysitter, you are responsible and practice safety precautions. Remember, when playing, safety is most important. Never endanger the child or yourself. Using the precautions listed and getting parental permission for the art and craft activities are important parts of safety. Equally important is that YOU participate and supervise the children during the activities.

Have fun and feel free to expand on these ideas. The children will look forward to seeing you again and again and their parents will be glad they chose you as their babysitter!

LET'S PLAY!
Jana & Gwen

GREETING THE CHILD

Most children need time to become accustomed to a babysitter, especially if the babysitter is new or infrequently seen by the child. When you arrive, familiarize yourself with the child's routine and home.

Show that you are happy to see and be with the child.

Speak softly to the child, especially babies.

Speak directly to the child by getting down to the child's eye level.

Listen to what the child has to say — be interested — ask questions.

Talking and playing with the child before the parents leave can make the separation easier.

HINT: Bring your own busy bag, described on page 15.

CHOOSING AN ACTIVITY

By using this guide you are choosing activities that are appropriate for the child's skill level.

When caring for children of different ages and abilities, look for activities that can be done with various skill levels. More than one block will be shown.

SKILL LEVELS: Infants up to babies able to sit without support

Sitting without support up to beginning walkers

Walkers up to good talkers

Older preschool through young school-age children

HINT: One effective way to work with an age difference of three years or more, is to have the older child be your helper. Let the older child help prepare and set up the art and craft projects or be your assistant in playing with the younger child.

BEGINNING TO PLAY

Being familiar with an activity before going on the job can be helpful, especially when managing various ages and larger groups of children. The index lists activities for larger groups.

Begin playing by talking to the child and suggest a couple of fun ideas for play. Let the child choose. Be flexible — if the child suggests something other than your ideas, consider them if they are appropriate for the child.

When a child becomes restless, it is time to stop the game or activity and do something else. Consider changing the type of play. A quiet activity such as reading might be followed by a more active game like Treasure Hunt.

A baby shows he or she is tired of the game by breaking eye contact and looking away. Let the baby rest before continuing or choosing another game or activity.

BUSY BAG

Bringing something with you that is new to the child can open the door to fun. Young children may enjoy a puppet or stuffed toy that can "talk" to the child each time you visit. Many older children are delighted by a prop or something already prepared for a craft project, such as those found in Section 3.

A good way to carry that special something is to use a BUSY BAG. A busy bag can be a tote bag, backpack, pillowcase or even a paper sack. A busy bag allows you to include other items such as a favorite storybook, playing cards, Couch Characters (page 46). Don't forget your HEY BABYSITTER, LET'S PLAY! activity book and information kit. You and your busy bag will be a welcome sight for any child you visit.

HINT: Jabber Jaws (page 118) is great to use when greeting the child. It only takes a few minutes to make and can help begin the conversation and set the mood for fun! Prepare it before you arrive and be sure to include it in your busy bag.

SECTION 1

Infant Games

SQUEAKS & WIGGLES

When you are playing with Baby, you are Baby's best friend and he or she will show it with squeaks and wiggles!

PROPS: A rattle or small toy that catches an infant's eye.

GAME: Hold the toy about 12 inches from Baby's face and slowly move it back and forth.
Talk or sing to Baby using the toy — mention color, noise, name of object, such as:

Little purple Teddy Bear says, 'Hello!'

Try this verse: Teddy bear, teddy bear, silly and funny,
Teddy bear, teddy bear, touch the tummy.
Teddy bear, teddy bear, show your knees,
Teddy bear, teddy bear, don't you sneeze!
Ah ... ah ... ah ... chooo!

For more verses to use while playing this game, see Finger Plays and Songs, pages 36 - 39.

E.V.: Visual tracking, attention span, rhythm

BABY OPERA

Babies love to hear singing and are the greatest critics. Don't hesitate to sing.
They always give rave reviews!

PROPS: Any baby toy may be used.

GAME 1: While raising and lowering the pitch of your voice, raise and lower a toy to correspond.

GAME 2: Without using a prop and speaking directly to the baby say:

La, La, La, La, La
Ma, Ma, Ma, Ma, Ma
Da, Da, Da, Da, Da
Ka, Ka, Ka, Ka, Ka
Pa, Pa, Pa, Pa . . . . . . PRECIOUS!
(Babies like the puff of air when the word precious is said!)

Remember: Keep motions slow and noise soft.

E.V.: Auditory discrimination, beginning sounds, attention span

BABY FITNESS

When Baby is getting restless, or just in need of a change of pace, try a little workout!

BEGIN: While Baby is lying on a flat surface such as the floor, gently hold and move Baby's arms, then legs, to the different motions that Baby likes. <u>Never force Baby</u>. Do not over extend arms or legs. Only play if Baby allows his or her arms or legs to be moved by gentle touch.

UPPER BODY: Say these words while doing the motions:

UP	Raise arms up by head.
DOWN	Lower arms by sides.
IN	Cross hands over chest.
OUT	Extend arms out at sides.

Repeat the above four motions two times, then say:

BOUNCE	With arms in down position, raise hands a couple of inches
BOUNCE	and lower back down to flat surface three times.
BOUNCE!	

Try the finger play, "Open, Shut Them," found on page 36. Use Baby's arms instead of hands.

LOWER BODY: Say these words while doing the motions.

Routine 1:   BICYCLE, BICYCLE, . . .   C O A S T, C O A S T

Holding ankles, move legs in a bicycle motion, stopping in different positions and saying coast.

Routine 2:   MARCH - ING, MARCH - ING

MARCHING, MARCHING, MARCH - ING

RUN, RUN, RUN, RUN, RUN, RUN, RUN

Hold ankles and move knees alternately toward chest. Marching movement is done slowly and running movement is done quickly.

E.V.: Gross motor, rhythm

GIGGLE, GIGGLE

Everything is new and exciting to babies. Touching is Baby's way to discover the world!

GAME: Gently touch Baby and say with rhythm:

Hands, hands, feet, feet,
knees, knees — TUMMY!   Gently touch tummy.

Nose, nose, mouth, mouth,
chin, chin — CHEEKS!   Gently touch cheeks.

Elbows, elbows, shoulders, shoulders,
ankles, ankles —— THIGHS!   Gently touch thighs.
Jana Sue Fitting © 1989

Slowing down the words and motions during the last phrase
will make this more exciting.

This is a fun game after diaper change.

E.V.: Identification, rhythm, anticipation

TICKLE BUG

When the moment's right for spontaneous fun, this is the game to play!

GAME 1:   Extend your arm over your head, with hand cupped like a spider,
          wiggle your fingers and say:

                    Where's the Tickle Bug?

          Gradually lower your hand, stopping a few times to build anticipation,
          and say:

                    Oh look, the Tickle Bug is coming to get you!

          Then gently tickle the child and say:

                                        Tickle, tickle, tickle . . . .

GAME 2:   Extend your arm over your head, with hand
          cupped like a spider and say:

                                        Push the button.

          When the child pushes an imaginary button,
          immediately drop your hand and gently tickle
          the child, saying:

                                        Tickle, tickle, tickle . . . .

E.V.: Anticipation, attention span

MIRROR MAGIC

It's great fun for you and Baby, as together you experience the magic of mirrors!

PROPS: A mirror.

GAME 1: Looking in the mirror together, say:

> Pat, pat Derek. (Baby's name)
>
> Pat, pat Sally. (Your name)

Gently pat the top of baby's head, then yours as you say names. Repeat a few times.

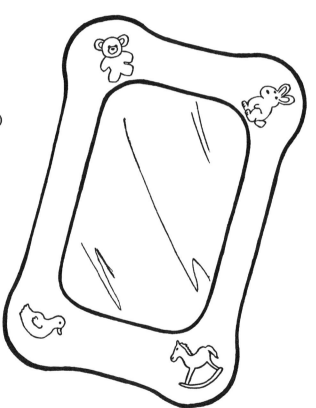

GAME 2:   This is a silly conversation game. Talk in silly voices and wave your hand or the baby's hand as you speak for each of you.

Hi, Derek, how are you doing?   (wave your hand)

Just fine, Sally. How are you?   (wave baby's hand)

Just fine. Bye, bye Derek. See you later.   (wave your hand)

Bye, bye Sally.   (wave baby's hand)

OR: Just say "Hi!" and "Bye!" and together move quickly in and out of the mirror.

GAME 3:   Ask the child to point out eyes, nose, mouth, hair, etc. — either theirs or yours — while looking in the mirror.

GAME 4:   Take turns making silly faces in the mirror. Show different feelings, such as: happy, sad, amazed, afraid, excited.

Remember: Use only a safe, shatterproof mirror if the child is holding it.
When standing in front of a wall mirror hold the child securely.

E.V.: Visual perception, self awareness

PEEK-A-BOO PLAY

There are as many ways to play Peek-a-Boo as there are people who play it. Here are some versions to get you started!

GAME 1: With baby laying on its back, cover your eyes with his or her feet and say:

> Where's Timmy?

A second later, gently move baby's feet from your eyes and say:

> Peeeeek-a-Boo!

This is often a good way to hear baby's first laughs. It is a good game after diaper change.

GAME 2: Peek around a piece of furniture or a doorway, and say:

> Timmy, where am I? or Timmy, where's Stephanie?

Then say:
> Peek-a-boo!

GAME 3:   This game can also be played with
a small towel or blanket. Just cover
your face and then PEEK! Holding
the towel in front of you and
peeking around the sides or under
it is fun too. Let the child remove
the towel.

Remember: Never leave the child or have the child out of your sight.
Always keep some part of your body in the child's view.
This should be fun and not scary for the child.

E.V.: Visual perception, anticipation

SECTION 2

Playing With Toys & Things on Hand

DRESSING THROUGH PLAY

This is a quick and easy way to put on jackets, sweaters and pajamas through play!

PROPS: Clothing the child is to wear.

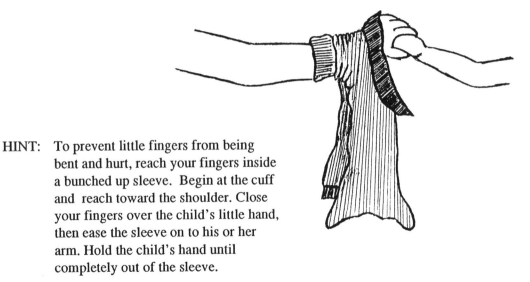

HINT: To prevent little fingers from being bent and hurt, reach your fingers inside a bunched up sleeve. Begin at the cuff and reach toward the shoulder. Close your fingers over the child's little hand, then ease the sleeve on to his or her arm. Hold the child's hand until completely out of the sleeve.

GAME: When putting on the jacket, say:

Where's the little left arm?

Where's the little left hand?

Then as you find them, say:

Hello left hand!

Hello left arm!

Hunt for the right arm and hand, left and right leg and foot, tummy, etc. Use the child's name when pulling on a shirt over the child's head and say "Peek" when the child's face appears.

See Button-Button (page 68) for a special bedtime dressing game.

E.V.: Identification, left and right discrimination

LAP GAMES

Active, but gentle motion is stimulating and exciting for the child.

PONY-BOY/PONY-GIRL

Have the child sit on your lap, facing you. Holding the child under the armpits, gently bounce him or her on your lap. While bouncing, say, in a sing-song way:

Pony-boy, Pony-boy, Won't you be my Pony-boy?

Don't say NO, here we go!

Far . . . a . . . cross . . . the . . . PLAINS !!!!

. . .Wheeeeeeeee!!!!

Giddy-up, giddy-up, giddy-up. Oh! My Pony-boy.
(Little girls like Pony-girl!)

Bounce your knees at an even speed until "Far across the plains". Then bounce slowly while at the same time dragging out the words. Then excitedly, say "Wheeeeee..." and raise your knees high with baby sitting on them.

THIS IS THE WAY. . . .

This is the way the ladies ride,
    LA - DE - DA - DE - DA   *Bounce slowly and gently.*

This is the way the gentlemen ride,
    LA - DA - DA - DA - DA   *Bounce more firmly and a little higher.*

This is the way the cowboys (cowgirls) ride,
    BOOM - BOOM - BOOM - BOOM - BOOM ! *While holding the child very securely, bounce him or her on your knees even more happily and higher.*

Remember: Hold the child securely when playing lap games, because most children squeal, laugh and wiggle with delight at this game.

E.V.: Anticipation, rhythm

WHERE'S THE BALL?

It's here, it's there, it's under the chair!

PROPS: Ball or small stuffed toy.

GAME: Have the child stand or sit a few feet away, facing you.
Gently toss the toy near the child telling him or her where it is,
such as:

> The ball is in front of you!
> The ball is behind you!
> The ball is by the chair!
> The ball is under you!   etc.

Then say:

> Get the ball. Throw (or bring) it back to me.

Other good words to use: over, beside, left, right, above, below, in, out, up and down.

E.V.: Listening for a purpose, vocabulary development, gross motor

FINGER PLAYS & SONGS

These are well known verses that are especially fun because they have motions that go with the words. There are many versions to these finger plays. These are versions we use.

OPEN, SHUT THEM

Open, shut them. Open, shut them.
Give a little clap.
Open, shut them. Open, shut them.
Lay them in your lap.

Creep them, creep them,
Creep them, creep them,
Right up to your chin.
Open wide your little mouth
But do not let them in!

Using your hands, or the child's, perform the motions.

Author Unknown

THUMBKIN

Where is Thumbkin?
Where is Thumbkin?
Here I am.
Here I am.
How are you today, sir?
Very well, thank you.
Run and hide.
Run and hide.

Begin by hiding your hands behind your back. Bring one fist forward with each "Here I am" line. Move your thumbs to "talk," then hide your hands behind your back again. Continue the verse using other fingers by substituting : pointer, middle man, ringer and pinky for Thumbkin.

Author Unknown

TWO LITTLE BLACKBIRDS

Two little blackbirds sitting on a hill,
One named Jack,
One named Jill.
Fly away Jack,
Fly away Jill,
Come back Jack,
Come back Jill.

Begin by hiding your hands behind your back. Hold up one index finger when each blackbird is named. Then hide your hands, one at a time, behind your back when they fly away. Again hold up one index finger as each backbird comes back.

Nursery Rhyme

ONE IS A CAT

One is a cat that says meow,
Two is a dog that says bow-wow,
Three is a crow that says caw-caw,
Four is a donkey that says hee-haw,
Five is a lamb that says baa-baa.

Six is a sheep that says maa-maa,
Seven is a chick that says cheep, cheep,
Eight is a hen that says cluck-cluck,
Nine is a cow that says moo-moo,
Ten is a rooster crowing Cock-A-Doodle-Doo!

Hold up a corresponding number of fingers as you say each line. Imitate a rooster as you say the last line.

Author Unknown

APPLES

Way up high in the apple tree,	*Raise hands overhead.*
Two little apples smiled at me.	*Smile.*
I shook that tree as hard as I could,	*Shake arms.*
And down came the apples.	*Drop one arm and then the other.*
Mmmmm were they good!	*Rub your tummy!* Author Unknown

LITTLE BUNNY FOO FOO

Little Bunny Foo Foo,
Hopping through the forest.
Picking up the field mice and
Bopping them on the head.

Down came the Fairy Godmother,
And she said:

Little Bunny Foo Foo,
I don't want to see you,
Picking up the field mice and
Bopping them on the head.

I'll give you **three** chances, then
I'll turn you into a GOOSE!

Repeat the first three stanzas, then:

I'll give you **two** more chances, then
I'll turn you into a GOOSE!

Repeat the first three stanzas, then:

I'll give you **one** more chance, then
I'll turn you into a GOOSE!

Repeat the first three stanzas, then:

You have **no more** chances.
I'll turn you into a GOOSE!
POOF! You're a GOOSE!!

Author Unknown

MORE FINGER PLAYS & ACTION SONGS

Bingo
The Bus Song
Do Your Ears Hang Low
Eensy Weensy Spider
The Farmer in the Dell
Going on a Lion (Bear) Hunt
Here is the Church
Head & Shoulders, Knees & Toes
Hickory, Dickory Dock
I'm a Little Teapot
London Bridge
The Muffin Man
The Mullberry Bush
Pat-A-Cake
Ring Around the Rosy
Ten Little Indians
This Little Piggy
This Old Man

FAVORITE SONGS

Alphabet Song
The Ants Go Marching
Hush, Little Baby
I've Been Working on the Railroad
Mary Had a Little Lamb
Old MacDonald
Old Susanna
Pop Goes the Weasel
Row, Row, Row Your Boat
Twinkle, Twinkle Little Star

E.V.: Vocabulary development, memory skills

DANCING AND MARCHING

When restlessness strikes, this game can march them off to fun!

PROPS: Any music with a strong beat. Records and cassettes work well because there are fewer interuptions, although a radio can be used too. Be sure to get permission and instructions before using equipment.

PREP: Begin the music. Gather "instruments" if desired.

GAME 1: Let the child dance and move with the music. The child may enjoy dancing with you too. Turn him or her around occasionally and show different ways to move their arms, legs, etc. to the music.

Babies love to be held close while you dance to gentle music. This may comfort baby.

Toddlers can dance and delight in moving on their own to music too.

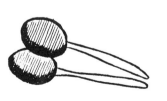

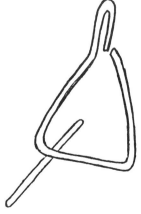

GAME 2: Parade and march around the room. You, the child and a stuffed animal can make a whole parade! Take turns being the drum major — this is especially fun with more than one child. Follow the leader is a good way to begin. Play instruments while marching.

SUGGESTED INSTRUMENTS

Imaginary: drum, cymbals, trumpet, trombone, flute, guitar
Toy: drums, tambourines, bells
Pretend: two small pillows could be soft cymbals, a pail or book could be a drum

GAME 3: For extra excitement, other props such as balloons and streamers may be used. Decorate bikes, strollers and wagons for outdoor parades!

E.V.: Gross motor, rhythm, creative play

DISCOVERING THE MAGICAL WORLD OF READING

Developing a lifetime love of reading begins early in life — even babies show interest and delight when being read to!

PROPS: A favorite book.

 Select a book with simple pictures and bright colors. Picture and animal books are favorites of small children. A puppet or stuffed animal may help tell the story.

Hold or rock the baby while reading. Don't read the book word-for-word. Simply point out different objects in the pictures. Older babies like to share what they know. Ask them to point to different things as you name them.

Whenever possible, imitate the sounds of the objects in the pictures. If animal books are used, imitate the animal's sound — babies love it!

Young children enjoy short stories. He or she may have a favorite book or you may select one with few words. Be prepared, many children like to hear the same story over and over.

Encourage the child to participate in story telling. Let the child guess what is going to happen next or ask why something happened.

"What do you think Little Miss Muffet said when she saw the spider?"
"Why do you think she said that?"
"What would you say?"

Older children may request longer stories or ones of particular interest to them. It's great when a child tries to help you read or stops and asks questions along the way.

Remember: Reading is fun and there is more than one way to enjoy a book.

E.V.: Vocabulary development, listening for enjoyment, word association, attention span

PICTURE RIDDLES

Open the door, guess what you see. Could it be quills or perhaps a pine tree!

PROPS: A manila folder or a large sheet of paper folded in half, scissors, a magazine or storybook with one subject pictured per page.

PREP: Cut doors in one side of the folder or folded paper. Slide the folder or folded paper over the page with the picture on it. Upon opening the door, a portion of the picture will be revealed.

GAME 1:   Have the child open one door at a time and guess what the hidden picture might be. Try asking the child:

What could this be?

The doors may have numbers on them. When playing with more than one child, have the children alternate guesses and doors on the same page.

Where could this picture have been taken?

E.V.: Observation, visual perception, identification

COUCH CHARACTERS

LIGHTS! CAMERA! ACTION! With you as the director, and the child as the audience, any couch becomes a stage for "Couch Characters"!

PROPS: A coloring book, magazine or catalog, scissors, cotton balls and glue. Markers, paint and crayons are optional.

PREP: Cut out a character from one of the sources listed, or cut out a face from a magazine and glue it to a figure you have drawn.

Carefully glue a small piece of cotton ball to the back of the character's head. The cotton ball will allow you to hang the characters on the front of a couch or other upholstered fabric. Felt may be used instead of a cotton ball. These steps may be completed ahead of time and included in your Busy Bag.

> Important: Let the glue dry completely before using the characters on a couch.
> Be sure to get parents' permission before using glue.

GAME 1: Use the characters to perform a little "play" for the child. Simple nursery rhymes are an easy way to begin. A boy and a girl character could be used to perform:

Jack and Jill   Little Miss Muffet
Jack Be Nimble, Jack be Quick   Jack in the Box

Additional props such as a pail, candlestick or spider can also be made.

GAME 2: Familiar simple stories can be used. Take turns staging the play by reading from a storybook.

GAME 3: Together, you and the child can make up your own story.

Note: Some children have the most fun making the characters and never get to the story. That's O.K.!

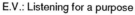

E.V.: Listening for a purpose

SAFARI HUNT

Children love adventures. Through imagination, Safari Hunt can take a child to many lands.

PROPS: Stuffed or toy animals. Hide three or four for a young child, more for an older child.

PREP: Hide the animals. For the very young child "hide" the animals in sight, such as on a chair or in the middle of the floor. Hide the animals in more difficult places for an older child.

GAME 1: Have the child hunt for the animals. Help a young child find animals by leading him or her to the animals if necessary. Just remember to be surprised when the CHILD finds the animal! Pretending that you can't find the animal gives the child a chance to surprise you and will delight the child.

Remember: Don't hide the child's favorite animal or toy. Don't leave the child alone when hiding the animals. Instead, have the child cover his or her eyes while you hide the animals.

GAME 2: Counting and naming the animals after they have been found can be lots of fun.

GAME 3: Let the child hide the animals for you to find. Don't find them too quickly. Make it a great hunt!

GAME 4: Pick out different rooms, areas or pieces of furniture to represent forests, deserts, trees, water or whatever environment you would like. Begin by using two environments and add more as the child's skills grow. Then hide fish in water, monkeys and birds in trees, bears and deer in forests, lizards in deserts, lions and zebras on the savanna.

Next, try hiding the animals where they don't belong.

E.V.: Observation, classification, counting

HOLIDAY SHAPE HUNT

A tisket, a tasket, a Holiday Shape basket and many surprises to find!

PROPS: Paper, scissors, pencil, cookie cutters, basket or paper bag for each child, tape or stapler.

PREP: Using cookie cutters, trace (or draw free-hand) and cut out holiday shapes. An older child may help with this if you supervise carefully. Make several shapes for each child. To save time, trace one simple shape and cut several sheets of paper at once.

While you trace and cut, have the child decorate his or her own bag for collecting the shapes. A paper bag basket can be made by cutting a 2-inch strip off the open end of the bag and taping it over the opening to be used as a handle.

HINT: The shapes can be prepared before you arrive. Include them in your Busy Bag (page 15) to be used over and over.

GAME 1: Hide the shapes and have the child find and collect them in his or her basket.

When playing this with different age groups, designate different areas of the room for each child. For the younger child, you might hide his or her shapes on the floor. Take turns hiding the shapes.

GAME 2: Try making and hiding different shapes in different colors. Have the child count and identify those he or she finds. An older child can follow clues to find well-hidden shapes, such as:

You're cold. You're getting warmer. You're HOT!!!

E.V.: Counting, identification

GAMES USING BLOCKS

Blocks build a world of fun. Here are some ideas to build upon!

PROPS: Blocks, plastic bowl, bucket or waste basket.

GAME 1: While leaning over the back of a couch, have the child drop blocks, one by one, into a bucket. Have an older child close one eye. More than one child can play this at the same time if each has his or her own bucket and supply of blocks.

GAME 2: Build towers, roads and cities with the child. Talk about size, shape, color and number of blocks being used.

The most fun part of this game is knocking the blocks down!

GAME 3: By stacking blocks and adding a ball, you can bowl.

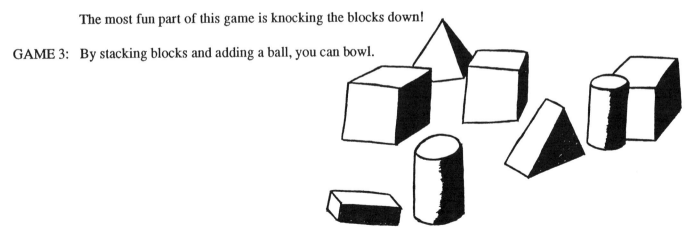

GAME 4:   Play "What comes next?" Using three blocks, arrange them in a simple pattern, such as:

red — blue — red   or   triangle — square — triangle

Have the child try to guess what color or shape will come next, or let the child try to match the pattern using his or her own three blocks.

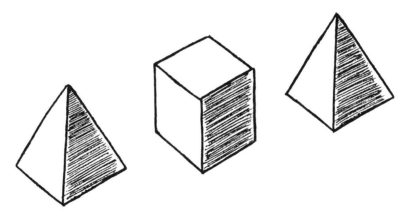

E.V.: Eye-hand coordination, counting, patterning, identification

DETECTIVE PLAY

The child plays detective as he solves a mystery with his power of observation!

WHAT'S DIFFERENT?

GAME: Have the child examine you. Then turn around and change one thing about your appearance. For example; put your collar up, unbutton one button, roll up a sleeve or change the position of your hair. The child then guesses what has changed.

Let the child try to trick you!

This can be lots of fun with more than one child. In this case, the person who guesses correctly has the next turn making the change.

WHAT'S MISSING?

PROPS: Three or four small toys or items on a tray, such as a cookie sheet.

GAME 1: Show the tray and its contents to the child. Have the child tell you what is on the tray. Have the child close his or her eyes or turn around while you remove something from the tray. Then have the child look again and tell you what is missing!

GAME 2: When playing with an older child, remove more than one item — eventually removing all of the items. When this becomes too easy add a few more toys.

GAME 3: Let the child have a turn and try to fool you.

Remember: This should be fun. Don't make it too difficult. Give clues until the child is successful.

E.V.: Observation, memory skills

JOKES AND RIDDLES

Children find humor in many things and love to laugh. Such silliness can be lots of fun for both of you!

PREP: None, unless you want to check out a joke or riddle book from a library to bring with you in your busy bag.

GAME: A younger child often prefers jokes that are simple and silly and may not make much sense. "Elephant jokes", "knock-knock jokes" and "Why did the chicken cross the road?" are some examples.

Riddles for a younger child also should be simple and silly.
Made up riddles such as:

What's sticky and purple and stays on bread?   (Grape jelly!)

often can be a real hit. Many children will want to make up riddles for you that may make little sense but are hilarious to the child. Encourage the child to do this and you will find yourself laughing too!

An older child often enjoys something a bit trickier, both in jokes and riddles. There are some good riddle and joke books for this age group that can be lots of fun.

Remember: Many of the riddles that may be old to you are brand new to the child!

E.V.: Creative oral expression, vocabulary development

CAMPING

When playing pretend, a child's imagination has no limits to the excitment and joy it creates!

PROPS: Use your imagination —
> ... a blanket can be a tent, sleeping bag, raincoat, sail for a boat
> ... blocks can be a campfire, groceries, fish, compass, rocks to mark a trail
> ... boxes can be pots, pans, lanterns, backpacks, flashlights, cameras
> ... cardboard tubes can be a telescope, binoculars, fishing pole
> ... a blanket, a pillow and the side of a couch or chair can be a lean-to.

PREP: None. You make it up as you go along.
Follow the child's lead. Encourage the child to make up part of the game.

GAME: Can include packing for a trip,
driving someplace, hiking, canoeing ...

At the campsite, you can set up, go
fishing, cooking, hunting for dinosaur
bones or arrowheads ...

PRETEND PRETEND PRETEND

Don't forget to take along stuffed animals
and imaginary friends, and have
rainstorms and snow ...

Try camping in a different time ...
the past, when dinosaurs were around ...
the future, and fly by spaceship to another planet ....

Hunt for lost goldmines and treasures ...

Sing around the campfire. See Finger Plays and Songs, page 39.

This game is as much fun outdoors as indoors. See Outdoor Adventure, page 80, for more ideas.

E.V.: Creative play

PRETEND PRETEND PRETEND

SHOPPING

PROPS: Boxes, paper cups, play dishes, containers, paper bags, baskets and whatever you are shopping for (even toy puppies, lumber, trucks, groceries, clothes, books ...)

GAMES: Can include making lists, traveling to shopping location (whether driving, sailing, flying ...) picking out and ordering items, phoning, paying, wrapping ...

Playing grocery store and shopping can be a fun way to talk about things that are alike and different. Why are certain foods located together? What things are in the freezer? Would you find peanut butter in a book store?

The salesman can come to you when he goes door-to-door. Home sales parties can be fun. Try serving pretend or real treats.

E.V.: Creative play, classification

BEAUTY PARLOR

PROPS: Yourself, comb, brush ...

GAMES: Boys as well as girls often enjoy combing, brushing and styling hair, especially yours! Pretend to put on make-up.

Make believe manicures — make fake fingernails (paper, crayons, scissors and tape). Toenails are neat too! Be silly, exaggerate!

E.V.: Creative play

ZOO

PROPS: Animals, dolls, pillows, boxes, blocks ....

GAMES: Place animals (even a picture book can be used) in different locations. For example, a couch can be the "Bear House" and have three different bears to be seen there.

Don't forget: hot dog and ice cream stands, making and selling tickets, having different "shows" like a dolphin show ....

When setting up and visiting the zoo — talk about which animals are alike and different, what they might eat, what kind of shelter they like, and what animals might "talk" about ....

Another way to play is to go on a safari to take pictures of animals in their natural homes.

E.V.: Creative play, classification

PRETEND PRETEND PRETEND

PUPPET SHOW

PROPS: Puppets, dolls, stuffed animals — items the puppet may use, such as small toys, cups, or books.
The stage can be the back of a couch or chair, or a large box.

PREP: Gather whatever you want for your puppet show. One doll or stuffed animal is enough.

GAME: Let the child become involved in preparing for the show.
Pick out a "stage."

The show can be a simple story or song familiar to the child.
Nursery rhymes work well. When Humpty Dumpty
(or Humpty Puppy, Humpty Dolly, etc.) falls off the wall,
the result can be lots of laughter.

Puppets are great magicians and can do wonderful disappearing acts!

Let the child put on the show. Be an enthusiastic audience.
Lots of cheering, laughing and clapping are well received!

Follow the child's interest. Setting the stage, complete with curtain, making and selling tickets, advertising and making posters can all be fun.

A pretend popcorn stand may be a fun addition for a puppet theater.

You can help the child make his or her own puppet. Puppets can be made from paper bags, socks, paper plates, etc. See Paper Plate Puppets, page 108.

E.V.: Creative play, creative oral expression

MEAL TIME FUN

Often a child is more interested in something if he or she has helped to create it.
This is especially true of food. Don't miss the fun of little helping hands!

PROPS: Appropriate utensils, food, dishes, etc.

PREP: Washing, cleaning, cutting or whatever is needed to prepare the meal or snack.
The child can help set tables, wash fruit and vegetables and show you where things are kept.
Don't forget to wash hands and preparation surfaces.

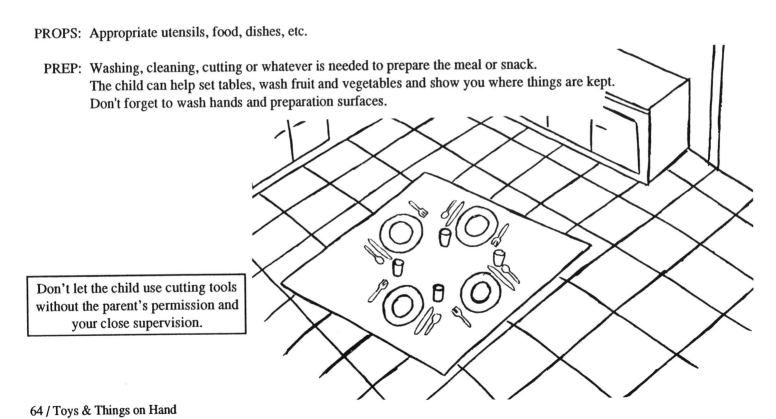

Don't let the child use cutting tools
without the parent's permission and
your close supervision.

GAME 1:   When having sandwiches, let the child choose a shape for
his or her sandwich: big or little triangle, circle, square or rectangle.
Then cut the shape or help the child do it. Cookie cutters are fun to use too.

GAME 2:   Picnics are lots of fun. Indoor and outdoor picnics are great.
Try one in the kitchen!

Remember: Serve bite-size pieces,
a couple at a time, to a very young
child to avoid choking.

E.V.: Eye-hand coordination, self-help skills

INDOOR SNOW FUN

When the child can't go out, let the snow come in!

PROPS: Clean, fluffy snow, cake pan, mittens, towel. Things to play with
in the snow, such as: a small shovel, cookie cutters, toy dishes.

PREP: Gather snow in the cake pan. Place a towel underneath
the pan. Have the child wear mittens or gloves so his or her hands
don't get cold.

GAME: Let the child play with toys in the snow. Mold shapes, build roads, make
snowmen, lakes or rivers.

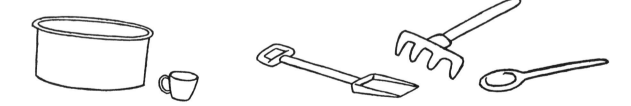

E.V.: Sensory awareness

BUTTON BUTTON

This game is designed to make the bedtime routine more fun.

PROPS: Object small enough to hide in your hand, articles of bedtime clothing or objects that could be used as bases, such as bed pillows.

PREP: Make a path between the child and the goal — the child's bed or a reading place, using bedtime clothing, such as pajamas, slippers, underwear or T-shirts, as the bases.

GAME: Have each child take turns guessing which hand the "button" is in. Put your hands behind your back to switch the object from hand to hand.

If the child guesses correctly, he or she may advance to the next available base and put on the piece of clothing. Continue guessing until the child reaches the goal.

The object of this game is to complete the dressing quickly and get on with the bedtime routine.

Once to the goal — begin the bedtime story!

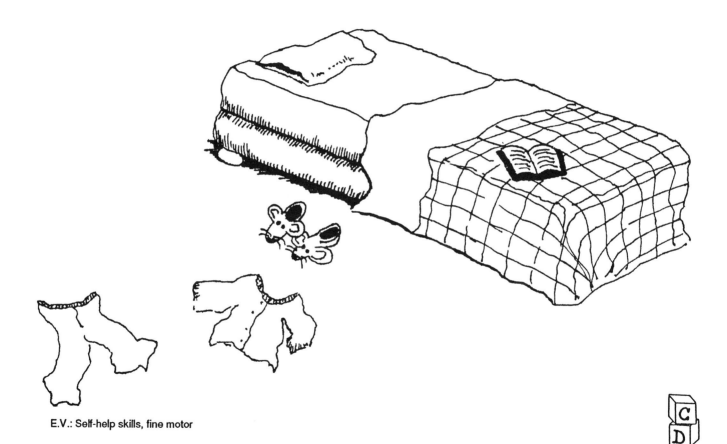

E.V.: Self-help skills, fine motor

SECRET AGENT (PICK UP)

Children love to help, and with a little imagination, work can be play!

PROPS: Toys and playthings that need to be picked up.

PREP: None. Just a fun and busy afternoon.

GAME: Each child becomes a "secret agent." Call to the child:

Secret Agent Brian, I have a secret mission for you.

When the child comes over to you, whisper in his or her ear a secret mission to pick up and put away something. Such as:

Your secret mission is to pick up the red blocks.

Keep the jobs small and easy to complete quickly. It is more fun to have many jobs to complete than a very big job. With more than one child, keep the "missions" (pick-up jobs) a secret from one another.

You should participate too. The child may like giving you secret missions.

In a short time everything will be put away. The child will be surprised and pleased at what he or she has done!

Try to save time after playing Secret Agent for a special story or a few minutes of quiet play.

E.V.: Self-help skills, classification

ABSURD STORY

Children have wonderful imaginations and this game can really get them started!

GAME: Make up a story that has mistakes in it. Two or three short statements can be enough. Encourage the child to correct you as you tell the story. Ask the child questions about the story to involve them.

For example:

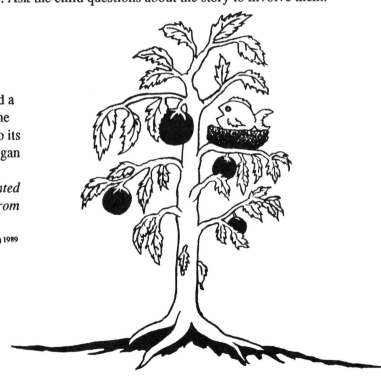

One day as I was walking through the woods, I heard a butterfly meow and saw the prettiest little fish fly up to its nest in a tomato tree. It began growling when a whale strolled by. *(I guess it wanted to scare the whale away from its nest.)* ....

Jana Sue Fitting © 1989

Or:

Last week at the zoo, we went to see the dinosaurs. My three favorites were the ones with black and white stripes and long trunks and very long necks. I especially liked their furry manes on their long necks. It made me laugh to see them swinging in the trees.

Jana Sue Fitting © 1989

NOTE: This is not as hard as you might think. Just make up silly things and soon you'll find this an easy way to entertain a child and yourself! Encourage the child to make up silly stories for you.

WHAT IF ...

skies were purple and birds could bark...
people had hoofs and trains had ears...
elephants could fly and snakes could run...
you could walk on the ceiling and rain fell up...

... is a fun way to follow up the story.

E.V.: Creative oral expression, listening for a purpose, classification

TREASURE HUNT

The hunt is on! Adventure is in the air when Treasure Hunt begins!

PROPS: Paper and pencil or pictures cut from catalogs or magazines and glue. Use these to make picture clues that show the child where to look. Use three or four clues for very young players; up to ten (or more) for older and more experienced players.

PREP: Draw or cut and glue pictures on paper. These are the clues. Hide them as in GAME 1 (below). Plan the final clue to lead to a "treasure," which may be an allowed treat or special story.

The clues may be added to your Busy Bag, page 15.

HINT: It is easier to work backwards by hiding the treasure first and then the clues.

GAME 1: Use these five clues: phone, plant, chair, TV, child's bed and treasure (storybook) for your treasure hunt. The clues and treasure can be hidden so that they are found in the following order.

FIRST: Give the child a picture of the phone (Clue 1).

Child goes to the phone and finds a picture of a plant (Clue 2).

Child goes to the plant and finds a picture of a chair (Clue 3).

Child goes to the chair and finds a picture of the TV (Clue 4).

Child goes to the TV and finds a picture of his or her bed (Clue 5).

Child goes to his or her bed and finds a favorite story waiting to be read.
(The Treasure)

Try to let the child find the clues by himself or herself, giving help when needed.
Remember, the idea is to succeed!

GAME 2: Older children enjoy more and also trickier clues. Riddles are fun to use too. Easy clues like "look in the red book" can build confidence in a beginning reader. Using the child's name in the clue is fun too, such as "Devin's bed." Non-readers will be happy to have the clue read to them.

A simple treasure map with an "X" to mark the treasure makes an exciting last hunt.

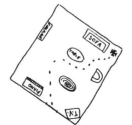

E.V.: Visual interpretation, order and sequence, word recognition

FISHING GAME

GONE FISHIN' has always been a great way to spend time. Here's a way to fish anytime!

PROPS: Fishing pole: a cardboard tube, ruler or yardstick and short length of string or yarn (about 15 inches long).
        Bait: a magnet tied to the end of a string (some magnetic letters work).
        Fish: pieces of paper cut to desired shapes (consider different shapes or letters, as well as fish shapes) , bobbie pin or paper clip, scissors, tape.

PREP: Tie or tape the string to the "pole" and magnet.
Cut out fish and tape or clip on a bobbie pin or paper clip to the "fish".
Tape more bobbie pins or paper clips to the "fish" for a young child.

GAME 1:   Have the child try to catch fish using the fishing pole.
Be sure to discuss the catch of the day.

"Oh look, Devin has caught six yellow hammerhead sharks, four blue turtles and a pink octopus with green stripes!"

For less preparation, try fishing for magnetic letters or numbers by using two paper clips hooked together as the "bait."

Remember: Keep ALL small
items away from and out of the
mouths of small children.

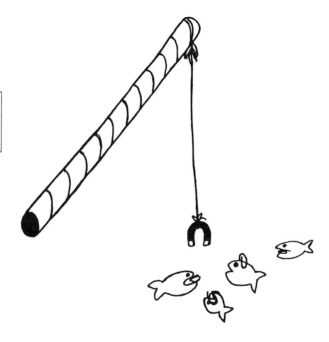

A small fishing pole and fish can fit in the Busy Bag, page 15.

E.V.: Eye-hand coordination, identification, counting

PAPER PLATE GAMES

Props needn't be elaborate, just a few paper plates is all it takes!

PROPS: 2 - 4 paper plates per child, crayons or markers.

PREP: Let the child color the plates using one color per plate. You might color them ahead of time and tuck them inside your busy bag! It's not necessary to color the plates completely.

GAME 1: Put the paper plates in a scattered pile on the floor. Walk in a circle around the paper plates, and sing: "Ring Around the Rosy"; replacing the last line of the song, "All fall down," with:

We all find red!

Have the child find a plate with the color named. Help the child find the correct match if needed. Once a plate has been found; you may return it to the pile, set it aside to be counted later, or have the child hold it on his or her head while singing the song and naming a new color.

Consider using numbers, letters, the child's name, shapes, or pictures of animals on the paper plates too. Pictures could be cut from coloring books or magazines and glued to the paper plates.

GAME 2: Play musical plates. Put the paper plates on the floor. Play music and have the child walk around the plates until you stop the music. Hold up a paper plate with a color, letter, shape, etc. on it. The child then quickly finds a matching plate and sits on it. With more than one child, make sure there are plates for everyone. It is fun to see who sits down first.

Instead of just walking, give the child different directions such as crawl, hop on one foot, walk backwards or skip to the music.

E.V.: Identification, gross motor

Outdoor Adventure

Turn an outdoor walk into an adventure by observing the world around you!

GAME 1: During a walk (to the park, around the block or in the backyard) have the child look for the following things:

> Different shapes and colors of leaves,
> Bugs, butterflies, worms or other insects,
> Animals or signs of their presence, such as tracks,
> Wild mushrooms, (warn the child not to touch or eat these),
> Sea shells,
> Wild flowers,
> Different colors, sizes, textures of rocks
> Or whatever your particular area may offer.

Listen for different sounds, such as:

> Birds,
> Frogs or toads,
> Squirrels,
> Crickets,
> Trains and planes,
> Car and truck noises.

Notice different smells and the feel of things too, such as:

> Moist, damp areas,
> Fresh pine scent,
> Different flowers in bloom,
> Scents of green plants, like mint,
> Smell of water: rain, ocean air, rivers, etc.,
> The coolness of shade against the heat of sun,
> Warmth of a brick building or a sidewalk.

GAME 2: Let the child go hunting in his or her backyard or at the park. Take along a plastic container to gather creatures found. Ask the child to try to identify the bugs, worms or other captured creatures.

Be sure not to hurt any creatures examined and to release them back to nature.

GAME 3: Have the child close his or her eyes. Then ask the child to describe what he or she can hear or smell or feel before opening his or her eyes.

E.V.: Sensory awareness, identification

IDEAS FOR OUTDOOR PLAY

Here is a list of games and activities well suited for outdoor play. Some may be familiar to you or they may bring others to mind.

Games: Tag   Activities: Bike Riding
             Kickball   Ball Catching
             Simon Says   Jump Rope
             Statues   Swinging
             Races   Blowing Bubbles
             Hop Scotch
             Red Rover   Action Songs: Ring Around the Rosy
             Red Light/Green Light   A Tisket, A Tasket
             Leap Frog   I'm a Little Teapot
             Freeze Tag   London Bridge
             Duck, Duck, Goose   Hookie Pookie
                                                        Follow the Leader

Outdoor Art: Crayon Rubbings
              Pretend Painting (bucket of water and a wide paint brush)
              Sidewalk Chalk Drawings, with permission
              Colored "Sand" (Recipe, see page 100)

CARD GAMES

Older children enjoy playing more "grown-up" games. Here's a list of some fun card games that you may know how to play!

Memory	Cards are arranged face down on floor and players take turns trying to make a match by remembering locations of cards. Also known as concentration.
Fish	Deal seven cards per player. Take turns asking for cards to match those in hand. Draw card from "fish" pile when you miss.
Old Maid	With a regular deck of playing cards, the queen of spades is usually the "Old Maid."
Spades	Four players - two partners. Spades is always trump. Each set of partners tries to guess number of tricks they can get. Score is kept.
Hearts	Four players - two partners. Involves passing cards, bidding, taking tricks and scoring.
Solitaire	There are many versions. Seven-card is well known. With two decks of cards, two people can play double solitaire by dealing their own game and playing on each other's aces as well as their own.

Don't forget board games, dominos and other favorite games the child may have.

SECTION 3

Arts & Crafts

HELPFUL HINTS

Arts and crafts need not be messy. By following these suggestions, just a few minutes are needed for clean-up.

1. Arts and crafts are best done in the kitchen, outdoors or an area specified by the parent.

2. The recipes are designed for a babysitter or parent's preparation. We suggest putting the mixing bowl in the sink when adding and mixing food coloring.

3. Cut open a paper sack and tape it to the table to be the child's own work station. When the child is done with the project, carefully roll up the sack and throw it away.

4. When the child is cutting paper, tape a paper bag to the edge of the table to be used as his or her very own scrap bag.

5. Have the child wear old clothes or protect his or her clothes with some kind of art smock, such as an old shirt, apron or towel. Check with the parent.

6. Using small amounts of clay or paint and a few tools, will help keep clean-up to a minimum.

7. Be sure to clean the child and the work area when done.

The materials for the art and craft projects are found in most kitchens. Make it a habit to inform parents of the project you plan to do. Ask permission to use their supplies and find out where they are located.

ART & CRAFT SUPPLIES

PAPER SOURCES

Construction paper
White freezer paper
Paper bags cut into sheets
Newspaper
Typing paper
Notebook paper
Wrapping paper
Aluminum foil

CREATIVE PAINT BRUSHES

Straws - blow through them or cut end to
    resemble a brush (dabbing will look like stars)
Cotton balls and swabs
Paint brushes, various widths
Fingers
Old sponges, cut up
String or yarn
Feather
Evergreen sprig (4")
Try wild flowers, weeds

PAINT CONTAINERS

Soft margarine lids and tubs
Aluminum foil cupped
Coated paper plates
Tin pans
Plastic foam meat trays
Plastic foam egg cartons

We recommend using flat containers and small amounts of paint because it is less messy, easier for little hands to work with and is not easily tipped over.

TOOLS FOR CLAY

Cookie cutters
Blocks with designs on them
Plastic drinking glasses (use for rolling and cutting)
Play dishes and cups
Rocks and leaves
Straws

SHINY PAINT

Shiny Paint is dazzling to the eye and pleasing to the tummy!

MATERIALS: Container for mixing paint, toothpicks, paper, creative paint brushes, see page 87.

1 glob	clear corn syrup, the size of a quarter
1 drop	food coloring

PREP: Mix the two ingredients completely, using toothpicks.

GAME 1: Paint pictures on paper. This paint does not dry thoroughly and may remain sticky indefinitely. Keep these painted papers from touching anything. This paint makes bright, colorful, shiny pictures. Be sure to try this activity!

GAME 2: Make edible finger puppets by using large marshmallows. Stick the marshmallow on the child's finger or on the end of a spoon. Paint faces on the marshmallows using shiny paint. Before eating, try a puppet finger play or song. See page 36 for ideas or make up your own.

```
Food coloring may stain.
Be sure to wipe up any drips immediately.
```

GAME 3: Paint peanut butter sandwiches. Instead of using jelly inside the sandwich, paint the peanut butter or the bread with shiny paint. You can cut the sandwich into different shapes for faces, etc. See Meal Time Fun, page 64. Try pancakes and graham crackers too.

Remember: If you are painting something to be eaten, be sure the painting tools are clean.

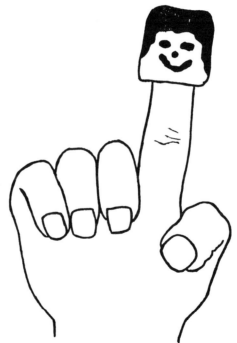

E.V.: Artistic expression, eye-hand coordination, fine motor

KALEIDOSCOPE PAINTING

This is a neat way to finger paint without getting fingers in the paint!

MATERIALS: Large self-sealing clear plastic bag, mixing containers, see page 87.   YIELD: 1 - 2 bags.

1/2 cup	flour
1/4 cup	salt
1/2 cup	water
2-3 drops	food coloring

PREP: Mix flour, salt and water in a small bowl. Using separate containers, divide the paint into the number of colors you plan to use. Add the food coloring and stir well. We recommend using at least three colors. One portion may be left uncolored (white).

Spoon the paint into different areas inside the plastic bag. Be sure to seal the bag securely, removing as much air as possible.

Food coloring may stain.
Be sure to wipe up any drips immediately.

GAME: Lay the sealed bag on a flat surface. Let the child experiment with the colors by pressing and moving his or her fingers over the bag. Squeezing can be fun too. When using more than one color, beautiful kaleidoscope effects can be achieved. The wonderful texture adds to the uniqueness of this paint.

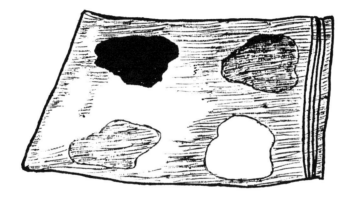

E.V.: Sensory awareness, artistic expression, fine motor

PERFECT PAINT

This paint may be used when store purchased paints are not available.

MATERIALS: Flat lid from a soft margarine container, toothpicks, creative paint brushes, see page 87.

1 glob	washable white school glue, the size of a nickel
1 drop	food coloring
A few drops	water, dripped from fingers, brush or straw

PREP: On the flat lid, mix the ingredients with a toothpick, straw, paintbrush or cotton swab until well blended.

```
Food coloring may stain.
Be sure to wipe up any drips immediately.
```

GAME: Experiment with creative paint brushes and paper at a tabletop work station.

HINT: Keeping the amount of paint to a minimum also keeps the mess to a minimum. A small coated paper plate can serve as a child's paint palette, which can be refilled as needed. See Helpful Hints, page 86.

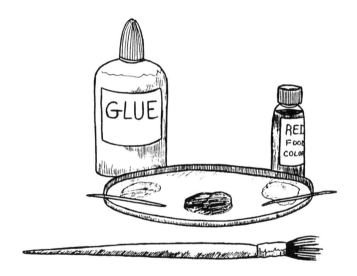

E.V.: Artistic expression, eye-hand coordination, fine motor

SOFT CLAY

This is a favorite of children and is good for hours of enjoyment!

MATERIALS: Two bowls, clay tools, see page 87, plastic placemat.   YIELD: 2-3 portions

1 cup	flour
1/2 cup	salt
1/4 cup	water
2 Tablespoons	vegetable oil
5 drops	food coloring (opt.)

OR:

1 small package of powdered children's drink mix (opt.)

PREP: Stir flour and salt together in a medium bowl. In a separate container, mix the water, oil and food coloring or drink mix, if used. Then add the liquids to the flour/salt mixture. Mix until mixture is like cookie dough.

```
Food coloring may stain.
Be sure to wipe up any drips immediately.
```

GAME: Working on a plastic placemat, let the child play using cookie cutters, blocks and textured surfaces for stencils, play cups and containers to cut with and shape around. Try making "snakes and worms".

E.V.: Artistic expression, fine motor

MOLDING CLAY (HARDENS)

This is the clay to use when you want to mold three-dimensional figures.

MATERIALS: Bowl, play clay tools, see page 87, plastic placemat, markers.   YIELD: 2-3 portions

1 1/2 cups	flour
1/2 cup	salt
1/2 cup	water

PREP: Mix these ingredients until it is no longer sticky and a smooth consistency is achieved.

GAME: Let the child create different shapes. Baby dolls, finger puppets, snakes, dinosaurs and alligators are some favorites. Markers may be used to decorate finished shapes. These creations may dry in one or two days.

E.V.: Artistic expression, fine motor

PEANUT BUTTER CLAY

A little baker can roll and cut out real no-bake cookies that may be served and eaten at teatime!

MATERIALS: Bowl, a few cookie cutters or clay tools, see page 87, plastic placemat.   YIELD: 2-3 portions

3/4 cup	peanut butter
3/4 cup	powdered milk
1/4 cup	honey

PREP: Mix ingredients in a medium bowl.

GAME: Let the child play with this edible dough on a plastic placemat. Raisins can be used for eyes, mouth, hair, etc.

E.V.: Artistic expression, fine motor

COLORED "SAND"

Pour, mix and experiment — a whole array of new shades can be created!

MATERIALS: Bowl, fork, paper cups, cookie sheet or cake pan.   YIELD: 1 portion

2 Tablespoons	salt
3 drops	food coloring

PREP: In a small bowl, thoroughly mix the salt and food coloring, using a fork. We recommend using three or more colors. Make one portion for each color.

GAME: Play with colored "sand" **outdoors**. Use a cookie sheet or cake pan to contain the "sand." Let the child use paper cups for pouring and spoons for mixing the different colors. Talk about how the colors change as they are mixed together.

Salt can harm grass and other living plants. When finished playing, throw away left over salt in a garbage container.

> Food coloring may stain.
> Be sure to wipe up any drips immediately.

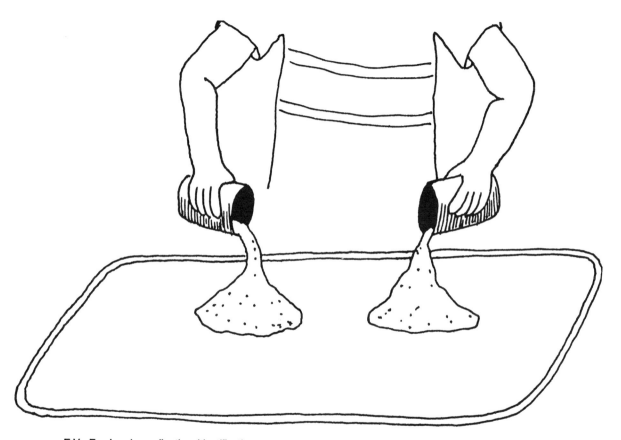

E.V.: Eye-hand coordination, identification

PUZZLES

Eeny meeny minny moe, can you see where this piece goes?

MATERIALS: Coloring book, cardboard (such as a gift box or cereal box), scissors, glue.

PREP: Choose a picture the child has colored or have the child color one. Hand-drawn pictures or pictures from magazines can be used too.

GAME 1: Glue the pictures onto the cardboard. Use glue sparely so you can begin cutting the pictures into puzzle pieces right away.

Three or four puzzle pieces are enough for a young child. Cut more pieces for an older child.

GAME 2: An older child may enjoy question/answer puzzles. Glue a picture on one half of the cardboard and write the name, or the first letter, of the pictured item on the other half.

You might divide the child's name, phone number or address between the two halves of a puzzle.

GAME 3: After the puzzle is made, play hide and seek with the puzzle pieces. Take turns.

See Treasure Hunt, page 74.

E.V.: Visual discrimination, visual perception, fine motor, eye-hand coordination

SILLY PICTURES

The sillier the picture, the more fun this will be! No drawing skills needed.

MATERIALS: Plain paper, pencil, marker or crayon.

GAME 1: Ask the child if he or she would like you to draw a picture. Have the child pick the subject. If suggestions are needed, try an outer space creature, octopus, dinosaur or the child. Draw the picture with your eyes closed. Be silly — have fun! Take turns.

GAME 2: Fold a piece of paper in half. You draw a face or figure on one half without showing the child. Then turn your drawn side down and have the child complete the picture on the clean side. Open and giggle!

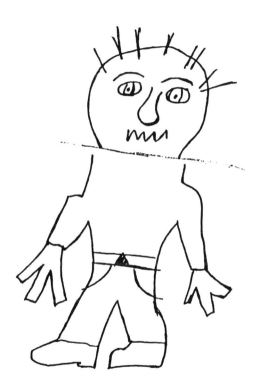

E.V.: Artistic expression, fine motor

MAKE YOUR OWN POST CARDS

Compliments are well received, especially when sent through the mail!

MATERIALS: Post card weight cardboard (a paper plate can be used), markers, stickers.

PREP: Cut out post cards 3 1/2 x 5 1/4 inches or use the pattern on the following page.

GAME 1: On the front side of the post card have the child draw a picture and or write a message, "Hi Granny!" use stickers, etc.

On the back print the mailing address. If made correctly, the post card can be mailed. Try mailing the child's post card to him or her.

GAME 2: For pretend, try using buckets or paper bags as mailboxes and let the child deliver or receive the mail. Envelopes with stickers can be used too.

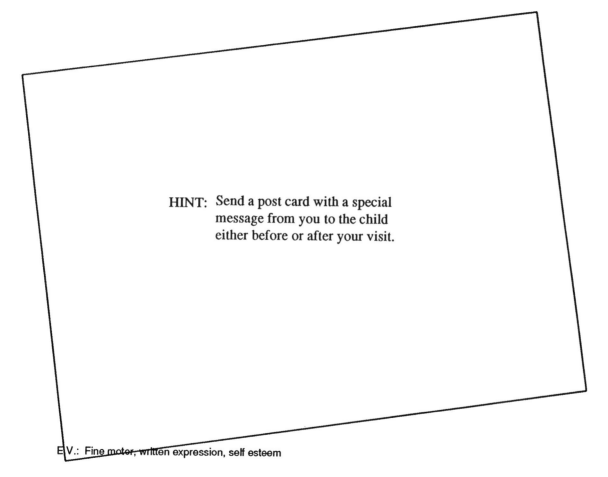

HINT: Send a post card with a special message from you to the child either before or after your visit.

EV.: Fine motor, written expression, self esteem

PAPER PLATE PUPPETS — HUMPTY DUMPTY

These are quick home-made puppets that are fun and easy to make!

MATERIALS: Paper plate (6"- 7" size or a large plate with the rim cut off), scissors, crayons or markers.

PREP: Help the child make the puppet. You should cut two holes near the bottom of the plate for child's fingers to poke through to be Humpty's legs.

Let the child color Humpty's face and clothes.

GAME: Once the puppets are finished, have the child use the puppets to act out the actions while reciting the "Humpty Dumpty" rhyme.

Humpty Dumpty sat on the wall,
Humpty Dumpty had a great fall,
All the king's horses and all the king's men,
Couldn't put Humpty together again!

Nursery Rhyme

HINT: Fold the paper plate where you want the finger holes to be, then cut half-circles to make the finger holes.

PAPER PLATE PUPPETS — FISH

MATERIALS: Paper plate, scissors, crayons or markers.

PREP: Cut three-fourths of the edge of a paper plate off (see picture). Then cut two holes in the lower part of the plate for the child's fingers to poke through to be the fish's fins.

GAME: Let the child color in the fish's face, gills, fins, etc.

When finished, you can use the puppets to act out fish stories or songs you may know. Wiggle fingers to make the fish swim. One cute song is "Three Little Fishies" by Saxie Dowell.

> Down in the medow in a little bitty pool,
> Swam three little fishies and a mama fishie too,
> "Swim" said the mama fishie, "Swim if you can"
> And they swam and they swam all over the dam.

E.V.: Fine motor, creative play

FASHION FIGURES

When the weather keeps them in, let their imagination take them out!

MATERIALS: Scissors, glue.
Figures: coloring book, magazine.
Clothes and accessories: wrapping paper, ribbon, crayons, markers.

PREP: Cut out figures of people or animals from a coloring book or magazine and glue to heavy paper or lightweight cardboard. You may wish to do this before you arrive and include them in your Busy Bag.

GAME 1: Have the child design his or her own wardrobe using suggested materials. Hats, gloves, boots, mittens and other accessories in addition to clothing can be made.

GAME 2: These may be used as paper dolls, puppets or Couch Characters, page 46.

GAME 3: Let the child try "sewing" clothes onto the figures as in Sewing Pictures, page 112.

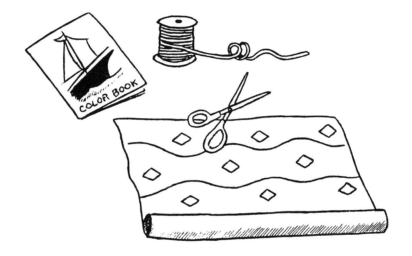

NOTE: See Paper Sources, page 87, for more ideas.

E.V.: Fine motor, eye-hand coordination, artistic expression

SEWING PICTURES

Sewing cards have always been a favorite with children. This is a way to make their very own!

MATERIALS: A picture colored by the child, heavy paper (large enough to glue the colored picture on), glue, scissors, long shoe string or yarn with the ends taped, paper punch (or use a ball-point pen to punch holes).

PREP: Glue the colored picture to the heavy paper such as a file folder. A plastic foam plate or paper plate works well for smaller pictures. Apply the glue thinly, so it will dry more quickly. Punch holes an inch or more apart around the outline of the picture. Make the holes large enough for the shoestring to pass through easily.

GAME 1: Let the child "sew" his or her picture by running the shoestring or yarn up and down through the holes.

GAME 2: Print the child's name on a blank piece of heavy paper. The child may enjoy coloring their name. Then punch the holes and let the child sew.

GAME 3: Have the child draw a picture. He or she might enjoy drawing a picture of himself or herself. Punch and sew.

GAME 4: Cut out a picture from a magazine and glue it to the heavy paper. Punch and sew.

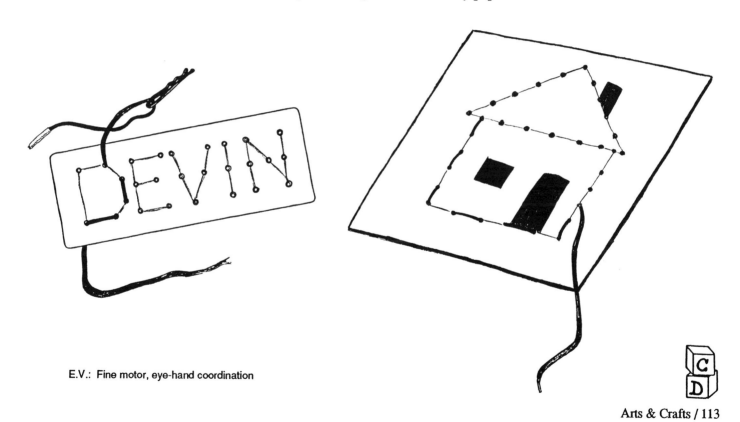

E.V.: Fine motor, eye-hand coordination

STRINGING JEWELRY

Little children like to wear jewelry. It's even more special when they've made it themselves!

MATERIALS: Circle-shaped cereal, straws (cut into pieces), beads made from cut-up egg cartons, yarn or heavy string, tape.

PREP.: Wrap a piece of tape around one end of the yarn or string to form a stiff "needle". For an older child, a bobbie pin also may be used.

Holes can be punched in egg cartons with a ball-point pen.

GAME: Let the child string the suggested items. You might show him or her different patterns, such as alternating two of one shape with one of another shape.

The whole string doesn't need to be strung. A few pieces of straws or cereals can make a great necklace. Jewelry makes a nice gift.

REMEMBER: Keep ALL small items away from and out
                        of the mouths of small children.

E.V: Fine motor, eye-hand coordination, patterning

LUNCH BAG KITES

This kite works. It runs on kid power — and kids love it!

MATERIALS: Lunch bag: crayons, markers or anything to use in decorating, tape
Tail: streamers, ribbons or paper strips (such as newspaper) one to two feet long
String or yarn: (maximum length 3 feet) used to pull kite

PREP: Let the child decorate a kite. You might suggest a theme, such as a bird, jet, butterfly, etc.

Tape kite tails to the bottom of the bag.

Put a piece of tape one inch from the open end of the bag (see picture). Punch a small hole through the tape, then thread the string through the hole and knot.

GAME: Playing outside, let the child fly the kite.

The really fun part of the activity is flying the kite. Decorating can be omitted.

CAUTION: Do not use plastic bags.

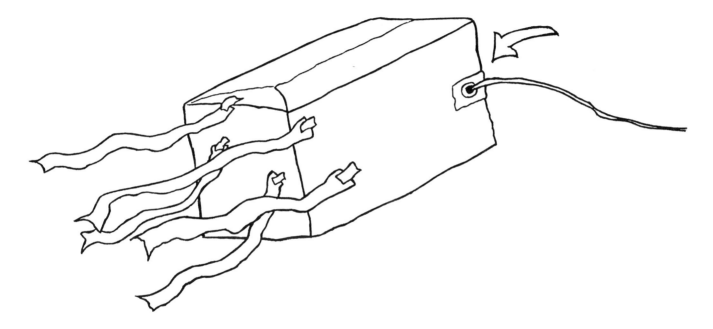

E.V.: Gross motor

JABBER JAWS

Using Jabber Jaws when first greeting a child can make a great first impression and set the mood for fun!

MATERIALS: Plain piece of paper (typing, notebook, etc.), crayons, pen or pencil

PREP: 1. Make a square by folding the top right corner diagonally down and lining up the edges of the paper.

2. Cut off the excess paper, leaving a folded triangle.

3. Open up the triangle. You now have a square.

4. Fold the top left corner down to meet the botton edge.

5. Open the triangle. You now have a square with two diagonal fold lines visible.

6. Fold the top right corner down to the center (where the fold lines cross).

7. Do this to the other corners.

8. Turn your paper over and repeat steps 6 and 7.

9. Number the eight sections, one through eight.

10. Open the numbered triangles and write messages under each number. Messages might be:

          I like you.   What kind of game do you like to play?

          We're going to have fun today.   Do you have a pet?

          You are funny.   Do you like to count?

          You're special.   What is your favorite story?

11. Fold the triangles back so messages are hidden and numbers are seen.

12. Fold the square in half, forming a rectangle.

13. Fold the rectangle in half, forming a small square.

14. Open the flaps, inserting index fingers and thumbs. Bring the points to a close at the top.

15. With points together, draw a silly face on the outside.

GAME: Ask the child a question about himself or herself such as name, age, favorite color, food, pet or sport. Spell or count out his or her answer by alternately opening and closing the Jabber Jaws.

Let the child choose a number inside and count it out. Choose another number and open the flap to find the special message to read to the child. Include Jabber Jaws in your Busy Bag, page 15.

E.V.: Self esteem

GLOSSARY of Educational Values

Listed here are the educational values denoted as E.V.: throughout the book. These are brief definitions of the terms as they apply to the activities in this book. There are other educational values that also apply. We have listed the primary educational values in each case.

Anticipation: to realize beforehand what is about to happen.

Artistic Expression: self expression through the use of art media, such as paint, clay and drawing materials.

Attention Span: ability to concentrate on a specific subject.

Auditory Discrimination: beginning attempts to recognize different spoken sounds.

Classification: separating items into different groups (i.e. animals/ environment) based on similarities and differences.

Counting: naming numbers in an increasing sequence.

Creative Play: a manner of play, based on original ideas, including role-playing.

Creative Oral Expression: original verbal communication, such as story-telling, made-up jokes and riddles.

Discriminative Listening: being able to recognize similar and different sounds.

Eye-Hand Coordination: ability to use sight in controling the fine movements of the hand, such as cutting on a line and putting puzzle pieces together.

Fine Motor: use of small muscles of the hand, such as in grasping and squeezing.

Gross Motor: use of large muscles of the body, as in running, jumping, crawling.

Identification: being able to recognize objects, such as shapes, colors, numbers, letters, body parts, sounds.

Left and Right Discrimination: distinguishing between right and left.

Listening for Enjoyment: listening for no purpose other than pleasure.

Listening for a Purpose: listening for specific information, such as the details in a story.

Memory Skills: developing the ability to recall what has been previously experienced.

Observation: noticing details.

Order and Sequence: following a logical series of events.

Patterning: recognizing and duplicating the order of a simple arrangement.

Rhythm: ability to hear or feel the repetition of sound or beat.

Self awareness: recognizing that oneself is a unique and separate being from the world around.

Self esteem: developing a positive self image.

Self-Help Skills: preparing for independent living by learning to accomplish such tasks as dressing and food preparation.

Sensory awareness: exploring the environment through the senses — sight, sound, smell, taste, touch.

Visual Discrimation: ability to see differences in shapes, size and color.

Visual Interpretation: relating a symbol for an object to the real object.

Visual Perception: ability to see a visual mental image of the whole object from an oral or visual clue.

Visual Tracking: developing an infant's ability to follow a slowly moving object with its eyes.

Vocabulary Development: learning and using new words, both written and oral.

Word Association: understanding that written words are symbols for spoken language.

Word Recognition: matching written words with their meanings.

Written expression: putting thoughts into written words.

INDEX

NOTES

NOTES

A Final Note

We would like to hear from you. Let us know your thoughts and ideas about **Hey Babysitter, Let's Play!** What do you really like and what would you like to see added? Your comments are important to us! You may write to the publisher at:

InQ Pub. Co.
P.O. Box 10
North Aurora, IL 60542

Other Hey Babysitter™ Products

Hey Babysitter Information Kit™
The vinyl folder contains a memo pad, phone message pad, emergency information card, babysitter business cards and a pen. The overall size is 6 1/2" x 9". Check for availability at your local bookstore, or order from the publisher. Include your name, address and zip code and write to the above address for more information and an order form.